W9-ASR-814

DATE DUE

TRADITIONAL TALES
from
ANCIENT GREECE

Vic Parker

Based on myths and legends retold by
Philip Ardagh

Illustrated by
Virginia Gray

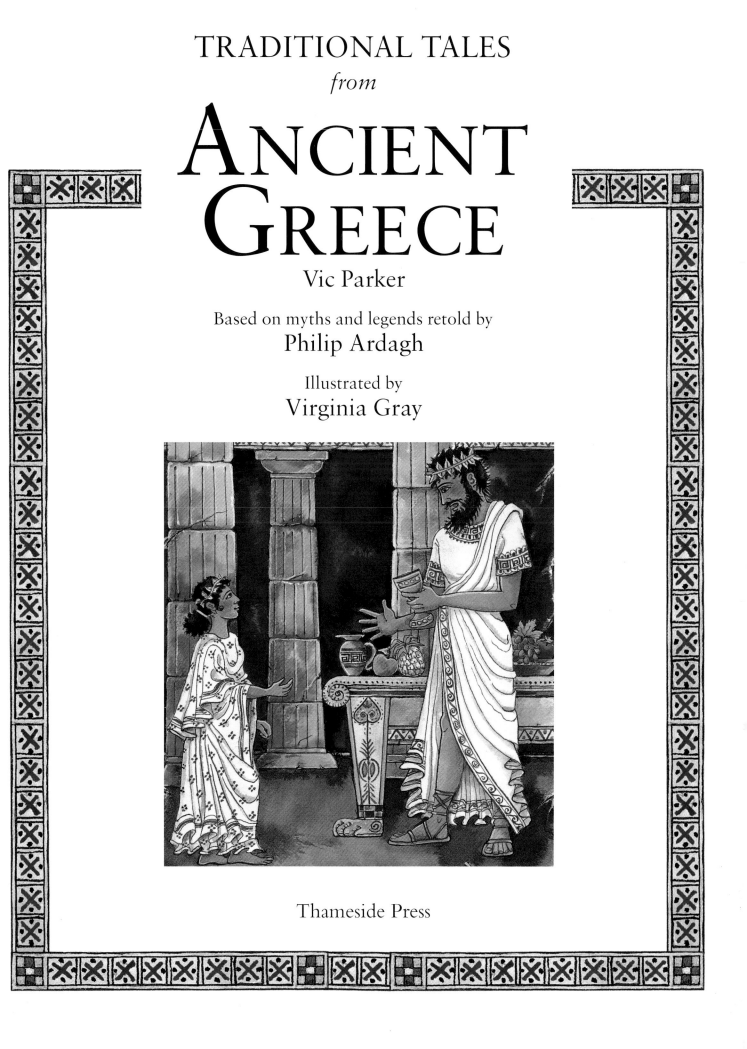

Thameside Press

Distributed in the United States by
Smart Apple Media
1980 Lookout Drive
North Mankato, MN 56003

Printed in the USA

Library of Congress Cataloging-in-Publication Data
Parker, Vic.
    Ancient Greece / by Vic Parker.
      p. cm.—(Traditional tales from around the world)
    Summary: A collection of myths relating the exploits and
    adventures of the gods and heroes of ancient Greece.
    ISBN 1-929298-72-2
      I. Mythology, Greek—Juvenile literature. [1. Mythology, Greek.]
    I. Title. II. Series.

BL782 .P28 2000
398.2'0938'01—dc21   00-022749

9 8 7 6 5 4 3 2 1

Editor: Stephanie Turnbull
Designer: Zoë Quayle
Educational consultant: Margaret Bellwood

CONTENTS

THE GREEK LANDS

**The stories in this book are nearly three thousand years old.
They were told by people who lived in Greece long, long ago.**

The Ancient Greeks sowed corn and grew olives in the Mediterranean
sun. They herded sheep up peaceful hillsides. They sailed boats from
island to island and cast their fishing nets into the sea. Then settlers
arrived from over the mountains and across the seas. The villages
grew into busy towns and cities. The cities appointed governments,
who laid down laws and built up armies. The army generals marched
their soldiers into foreign lands and took new territories. And so the
language, customs, and religion of the Ancient Greek people spread,
until they had an empire that was the strongest in Europe.

The Ancient Greeks thought that it wasn't just humans like themselves who lived in the universe. They believed that the world was filled with all sorts of magical beings.

There were beautiful spirits all around, in every tree and river and in every mountain and valley. These spirits were called nymphs, and most of the time they were invisible to humans.

There were strange creatures too, who were half-human and half-animal. Some were good and others were evil. There were also monsters and giants who lurked in faraway places.

The universe was ruled by gods and goddesses, who lived at the top of a mountain called Mount Olympus. They had superhuman powers, and the Ancient Greeks often prayed to them for help. Zeus, the king of the gods, controlled thunder and lightning. The goddess Athena had the power to help warriors win battles and wars. Poseidon was the god of the sea. He could stir up the wind and waves into terrible storms. Hades was the grim king of the underworld, ruler of the dead.

The Ancient Greeks also told stories about a few brave humans. These adventurous heroes went on dangerous journeys and performed all kinds of bold deeds.

The Ancient Greeks decorated jars and vases with pictures of gods, goddesses, and heroes.

THE GIFT OF FIRE

The god Prometheus was hard at work. He was creating a new race of beings. He molded the creatures and gave them life. Prometheus called them humans.

Prometheus decided to give his humans the gift of fire, so that they could cook, keep warm, and make metal soft enough to hammer into tools. But Zeus, the king of the gods, would not let him. Zeus wanted to keep the secret of fire for the gods. Prometheus thought this was unfair.

Secretly, Prometheus climbed to the top of Mount Olympus and waited until Helios, the sun god, flew past in his fiery chariot. Prometheus reached up to the flaming wheels and lit a torch of wooden sticks. He snapped off a burning twig and hid it inside a vegetable called fennel. Then the daring god hurried away to his humans.

That night, Zeus saw lights twinkling in the darkness all over the world. They were fires! In a fury, Zeus seized Prometheus and chained him to a rock at the end of the earth. Then Zeus ordered an eagle to peck and claw at the disobedient god's flesh. And there Prometheus stayed, waiting for the day when one of his humans would be brave enough to come and rescue him....

THE GOLDEN TOUCH

Dionysus, the god of wine, opened his eyes and stretched.

My! That was a good party last night, he thought to himself. His wild parties were famous. When Dionysus brought out the wine, everyone sang and danced and forgot everything except having fun.

"Oops!" Dionysus chuckled. "Even *I* forgot something last night. I left my friend Silenus at the party!"

The jolly god hurried off at once to look for him.

Luckily, a king called Midas had found the god's lost friend wandering around his royal gardens. King Midas had taken Silenus into his palace and looked after him.

Dionysus was overjoyed to see that Silenus was safe.

"I must repay your goodness to my friend," he thanked King Midas. "I shall grant you a wish!"

King Midas's face lit up with excitement.

"A wish!" he gasped. "For whatever I want?"

"For whatever you want," beamed Dionysus.

Midas thought hard, stroking his beard. There was a greedy gleam in his eye.

"I've got it!" he cried at last. "I wish for everything I touch to turn into gold!"

Dionysus roared with laughter.

"Are you sure?" he asked. "You may regret it!"

"I'm quite sure," said King Midas firmly.

"Then it is done," Dionysus announced, with a cheery wave of his hand. "But don't say I didn't warn you...."

Midas couldn't wait to try out his gift. As soon as the god and his friend had left, he stretched out his hand. *Crack!* The king broke a twig off a tree. At once it grew heavy and bright. It had turned to solid gold.

The king's heart began to race. He stooped and picked a flower. Suddenly he held a golden bloom in his hand!

Midas whooped with delight. He dashed around his garden, touching everything. *Ping!* Pebbles gleamed. *Zing!* Grass glittered. *Ting!* The fountain froze into a golden spray. Then he hurried into his palace. *Tap!* The floor shone. *Rap!* Pillars sparkled. *Zap!* Doors glowed.

Midas didn't stop until he had turned his whole palace into gold. It was hungry, thirsty work!

"A feast to celebrate my new fortune!" the king cried.

Servants scurried in, bringing plates piled with food and pitchers brimming over with wine. With a smack of his lips, Midas raised a chicken drumstick to his mouth.

"Owwwwww!"

He broke a tooth as he bit down on hard metal.

Midas reached for a goblet of wine to wash his mouth. But the wine hardened as soon as it met his lips.

The king pushed back his golden chair in dismay.

"I'd give everything I've turned into gold for just one gulp of water and one mouthful of bread," he groaned, pacing up and down. "How foolish I have been!"

Then Midas heard his golden doors creak open. He spun around to see his little daughter running toward him. Filled with horror, he tried to back away—but it was too late.

"Daddy!" she cried, flinging her arms around her father.

Tears streamed from Midas's face as he felt his daughter stiffen into a cold, golden statue.

Weeping bitterly, the king left his golden palace and golden garden, and searched high and low until he found Dionysus. Then the miserable Midas threw himself at the god's feet and begged him to undo the magic.

"I told you so!" sang Dionysus, wagging a playful finger.

Finally the god took pity on the wretched king. He told Midas to wash himself in the water of the River Pactolus. The moment the king did so, he found that the golden touch left him forever. And from that day to this, the sand of the riverbed has been a gleaming gold—a reminder to all greedy people of the trouble that riches can bring.

THE MAN WHO LOVED HIMSELF

Narcissus knew he was a good-looking young man. Wherever he went, people stopped to gaze at his handsome face and strong body.

"How beautiful you are!" they gasped in amazement.

Narcissus just glared at them coldly through his bright, sparkling eyes.

"Tell us your name!" they begged adoringly.

Narcissus just shrugged his broad shoulders, tossed his shining hair, and walked away.

People paid Narcissus so many compliments that he became big-headed. He refused to have anything to do with people who weren't as attractive as he was. And of course, no one was!

But the day finally came when someone caught Narcissus' attention. He was walking through a forest when he sensed that someone was following him. Narcissus looked around—but no one was there.

"Who are you?" he yelled into the silent greenness.

A silvery voice came floating back on the breeze.

"Who are *you*?" it sang to Narcissus.

The voice was so lovely that
his heart skipped a beat.

"Let me see you!" he called.

"Let *me* see *you*," the musical voice tinkled back.

It came from a timid wood nymph called Echo, who
was hiding among the trees. Echo had fallen in love
with Narcissus from the moment she had glimpsed him,
but she couldn't tell him how she felt. The poor nymph
could only repeat words other people spoke. This was
a terrible punishment from Zeus for talking too much.

Still, Narcissus was charmed by Echo's few words.

This woman thinks and speaks like me! he thought.

"Show yourself!" Narcissus pleaded. "Let me hold you!"

"Let *me* hold *you*," Echo whispered softly, and she
shyly came out from the trees.

Narcissus' face fell.

"A nymph!" he cried in disgust. "Why couldn't you
have been a goddess or a princess?"

And the arrogant young man strode away.

The sad Echo followed behind, tears rolling
down her cheeks. She watched as Narcissus
stopped by a clear pool and scooped up some
water to drink. Echo heard him gasp in amazement.

The loveliest face he had ever seen was peering up at him!

"At last I am in love!" Narcissus smiled, and to his joy, the face smiled right back.

Narcissus reached out his hand to the beautiful person. His fingers stirred the water and the face disappeared.

"No!" he cried in despair. "It's my own reflection!"

Heartbroken, Narcissus took out his dagger and plunged it into his chest.

"Goodbye," he groaned to the world as he fell.

"Goodbye," he heard Echo's voice sob back.

Narcissus died and his beauty faded away forever. But a tiny white flower sprang up from the spot where his blood dripped. We still call this flower narcissus today.

THE MONSTER IN THE MAZE

King Minos of Crete had a big problem. His wife had fallen in love with a bull and given birth to a monster. The baby was human from the neck down, but it had a bull's head—horns and all. Minos was so ashamed that he asked a great inventor called Daedalus to help him hide away his disgraced family.

Daedalus had a brilliant idea. First, he built the king a splendid palace. Then, deep beneath the palace, he built an underground chamber surrounded by a brilliantly complicated maze. Its tunnels twisted and turned and curled. Its paths led up and down and forward and backward and sideways. Every narrow corridor seemed to wind its way to a dead end. There was only one way in and out of the center, and only Daedalus knew the route. The genius called his maze the Labyrinth.

"Hide your wife and the monster in the middle of the maze," Daedalus told King Minos. "Lock the door tight and no one will ever see them."

Minos breathed a sigh of relief and threw his wife and her child into the murky tunnels, hoping to forget all about them.

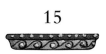

As the years passed, bellows of rage began to come from under the palace. People guessed that a monster was down there, and they spoke in whispers about a terrifying creature they called the Minotaur. Eventually the bloodthirsty howls started to frighten the king himself.

Things went from bad to worse when Minos found out that his favorite son had been murdered by some thugs from the city of Athens. But as the sorrowful king sat on his throne with his head in his hands, he suddenly had an idea—a brilliant way of punishing the people of Athens *and* keeping the Minotaur quiet....

Minos ordered King Aegeus of Athens to pay for the death of his son. But Minos did not ask for money—he wanted human lives. He told King Aegeus that he must send him seven young men and seven young women every nine years, or he would start a war. King Aegeus of Athens had no choice.

It wasn't long before fourteen nervous men and women came sailing into Crete. Their ship was rigged with grim, black sails instead of airy, white ones, as a sign of deep sorrow. The next day, the delighted King Minos locked the terrified young people in the Labyrinth. He closed his ears to their pleas and walked away, rubbing his hands in glee. The Minotaur would hunt down the helpless victims.

Once the beast had enjoyed its tasty supper, it would be quiet and content for a while....

Back in Athens, King Aegeus was horrified when he heard what had happened to his people. But nine years passed and he could think of no way out of the deadly bargain. He had to send a second black-sailed boat to Crete. After nine more years he had to do the same again. With a heavy heart, the king asked for more volunteers to sail to their terrible deaths.

As the first brave man stepped forward, the king's blood ran cold. It was his own son, Theseus.

"Don't worry, Father," Theseus whispered. "I promise that I will return—and I will bring my thirteen friends home with me, too."

The king hugged his son.

"I shall watch and pray for you every day," he sobbed. "I beg you, if you are on the boat when it returns, replace the black sail with a white one. Then, when I see it coming, I shall know at once that you are safe."

So the third black-sailed boat sailed for Crete. It was met in the harbor by King Minos, with his beautiful daughter, Ariadne, at his side. As soon as Ariadne caught sight of Theseus, she fell deeply in love.

That night, Ariadne crept in secret to Theseus's chamber.

She found him pacing back and forth, trying to think of a plan to defeat the Minotaur. Ariadne pressed a finger to her lips and silently led the surprised Theseus to the door of the Labyrinth.

"I can show you a way to kill the monster," she whispered. "But only if you promise to take me back home with you to be your wife."

"I promise," Theseus nodded.

"Then take these," Ariadne urged, pressing a sword and a ball of thread into Theseus's hands. "This thread is magic. It was given to me by the inventor of the maze himself. Tie the loose end around the doorknob and then drop the ball. It will lead you to the Minotaur."

Ariadne quickly planted a kiss on Theseus's lips.

"Now go," she said, blushing. "I will gather your friends and we will wait for you at the boat."

She unlocked the Labyrinth door and slipped away into the palace.

Theseus swallowed hard. He gripped the sword tightly. Then he tied the thread around the doorknob and dropped the magic ball onto the floor of the maze.

At once, it rolled away into the gloom, unraveling as it went. Theseus hurried after it, ducking through low passages and zigzagging through right and left turns.

The smell of rotting flesh hung in the air, growing stronger by the second. Suddenly Theseus turned a corner and found himself in a large room. He nearly ran right into a creature asleep on the floor—it was the Minotaur!

The half-man, half-beast lay sprawled across a heap of pale sticks. With horror, Theseus realized that they were human bones! As he stood in shock at the evil sight, the Minotaur's wet nostrils twitched. It sniffed the air. Its blood-red eyes flicked open. It was wide awake!

With a great snort, the angry monster sprang up to rip Theseus apart. At once, the brave young man forgot his fear and jabbed out with his sword. He slashed the beast across the chest, and the Minotaur felt pain for the first time. It bellowed with rage and leaped forward once more. Theseus jumped nimbly aside, and the monster's strong arms grabbed thin air. As the Minotaur stumbled, Theseus raised his sword high above his head. With a mighty roar, he slashed down with all his strength. The Minotaur's head rolled onto the floor.

Without stopping for breath, Theseus spun around and picked up the thread. He followed it back to the entrance as fast as his legs would carry him.

Theseus ran and ran, and didn't stop until he was out of King Minos's palace and down at the seashore.

Ariadne and his friends were waiting for him. In the pale moonlight, they jumped aboard their boat and sailed away.

But in his haste Theseus forgot one very important thing. He didn't remember to take down the black sails and put up white ones.

When King Aegeus saw the black-sailed ship returning to Athens, he howled in despair.

"My brave son is dead!"

The sorrowing king never found out that Theseus was a hero, alive and well. In his grief, King Aegeus threw himself over a cliff and drowned in the swirling waves below. And from that day to this, the sea has been called the Aegean, in memory of him.

The Boy Who Flew Too High

King Minos of Crete was furious with Daedalus, the famous inventor of the Labyrinth. Minos blamed Daedalus for the whole problem of the Minotaur, so he locked up the inventor and his son, Icarus. Somehow the clever pair managed to escape.

The raging king ordered his guards to search Crete from top to bottom, but Daedalus and Icarus hid in a secret cave near the sea. The genius thought long and hard, and finally came up with a way to escape from the island. Daedalus's escape plan was risky—but with a bit of luck, he thought it might work....

The inventor began to trap hundreds of birds and set Icarus to work plucking their feathers.

"Why are we doing this, Father?" asked Icarus.

"You will find out in time, son," Daedalus replied, without even looking up from his traps.

When the feathers had piled up into a huge mound, the inventor finally allowed his son to rest. Icarus sank into a worn-out sleep, but Daedalus kept working.

He sewed feather after feather onto four large pieces of cloth, sealing them in place with drops of hot wax.

22

As dawn was breaking, Daedalus finished his task. "Wake up!" he urged his son. "It's time to go."

Icarus rubbed his eyes. Was he dreaming, or was his father holding two huge pairs of feathered wings?

Daedalus hurried his son outside and up onto the cliff top. Icarus peered over the edge. Far below, the sea crashed angrily on the rocks. It made Icarus dizzy to look at it, and he took a nervous step back.

Daedalus strapped a pair of wings onto his son's arms. He put on a pair too, and told Icarus how to fasten them.

"Tighter," Daedalus urged through gritted teeth. "Make sure they can't come undone."

"Are we really going to fly?" Icarus whispered, amazed.

"Yes, far away from this island," nodded Daedalus briskly. "But don't fly too high, near the sun, or too low, where the sea-spray will wet your feathers. Just follow me and do exactly what I do."

Daedalus led his son away from the cliff edge. The inventor shut his eyes and prayed silently to the gods. Then he looked at his son and smiled.

"Now!" he cried. "Run as fast as you can!"

Together, the father and son raced over the grass.

"Don't stop!" cried Daedalus, as the cliff edge loomed closer and closer.

Icarus shut his eyes and leaped into space. Suddenly he was falling....

"Spread your wings, Icarus!" called Daedalus frantically.

Icarus looked up to see his father gliding overhead, his feathered arms outstretched. With the wind whistling past his ears, Icarus struggled to open his own wings wide. As if by magic, he felt himself lifted on a cushion of air. Up and up and up he went—until at last he was floating behind his father on the breeze.

Icarus began to smile.

"We did it!" he whispered to himself in delight.

Far, far below them, the green of the island had given way to the blue of the sea. They were out of danger!

"Whee!" Icarus cried, beginning to enjoy the feeling of weightlessness. He lifted his head and flew higher. He didn't realize he was leaving his father far below.

"I can go anywhere I choose!" Icarus yelled. "I can fly right up to the sun!"

Icarus soared upward and hovered in the heat. The sun was so beautiful—more huge and fiery than he had ever imagined.

"I'm free as a bird!" Icarus sang.

Suddenly his joy turned to pain as hot wax began to run down his arms.

"My wings are melting!" the boy yelled in panic.

Feathers began to flutter past Icarus one by one . . . then in clumps . . . and with a bump, then a jolt, Icarus began to fall.

"Help!" he cried at the top of his voice. "Father, help!"

The boy's voice carried on the wind to where Daedalus flew, far out in front. The inventor looked back in horror, but there was nothing he could do to help.

"*No!*" Daedalus moaned in despair, as he saw his son tumble through the air and land with a splash in the sea.

And as the inventor flew on to freedom, his tears fell from the skies like rain.

THE WINGED HORSE

Bellerophon was an ordinary young man. One night he saw a wonderful sight—a magical horse drinking at a spring. The animal was smooth and sleek and as white as snow. But most marvelous of all, it had wings! Bellerophon gasped out loud, startling the horse. The frightened creature leaped into the sky and flew into the clouds that drifted across the moon.

Bellerophon longed to own the amazing horse. Then he had a dream in which the goddess Athena appeared.

"The horse is called Pegasus," Athena said, and she handed Bellerophon a golden bridle. "Use this and he will be yours."

Bellerophon woke with a start. To his joy, he found that he really did have a golden bridle!

He hurried back to the spring to wait for the horse. Soon he heard beating wings thudding through the inky, blue sky. A shiver went down his spine as Pegasus appeared and landed by the spring. The horse dipped his head to drink, and Bellerophon nervously crept forward. Pegasus whinnied, but stood still and let Bellerophon throw the golden bridle over his head. They were friends.

With the help of Pegasus, Bellerophon had all kinds of adventures and performed many brave deeds. He even killed the Chimera, a fierce fire-breathing monster. People far and wide told tales of the hero and his magic horse.

Fame soon went to Bellerophon's head. He felt so important that he decided to go and live with the gods.

Zeus, the king of the gods, was outraged. As soon as he saw Bellerophon flying near Mount Olympus, he sent a horsefly to bite Pegasus. The horse reared up in pain, sending Bellerophon tumbling to the earth.

Without his winged horse, he had to live the rest of his life as an ordinary human. Pegasus is still among the gods, carrying Zeus's thunderbolts on his back.

Heracles, Hero of Heroes

Like all young men, Heracles wanted to join the gods of Mount Olympus. For his friends, this was nothing more than a wild daydream, but for Heracles it was a real hope. Even though his mother was a human, his father was the mighty Zeus himself, the king of the gods! Heracles had been born with superhuman strength and courage. When he was only a baby, he had squeezed two snakes to death in his chubby fists. Since then Heracles had grown into the strongest, bravest young man in all of Greece.

Zeus was very proud of his human son and planned to make him the king of Mycenae, but Zeus's goddess wife Hera had always hated Heracles. (In fact, it was Hera who had sent the two snakes to attack Heracles when he was a baby.) So she cunningly spoiled things by crowning another man the king of Mycenae instead.

Zeus was furious. He stormed around Mount Olympus in a terrible rage, yelling like thunder and hurling spears of lightning. The only way that Hera could calm her angry husband was to agree to let Heracles become a god.

But she insisted on one condition. Heracles would have to prove that he was worthy by carrying out twelve tasks, called labors. The tasks were to be set by the king of Mycenae.

Zeus agreed, and the crafty Hera hurried away to pay the king of Mycenae a secret visit. She planned to tell the king each of the challenges that he must give Heracles—tasks that she was sure were impossible.

Heracles will never succeed! Hera smirked to herself.

The first thing the king ordered Heracles to do was to kill a ferocious lion so big and tough that weapons couldn't even scratch its skin. The fearless hero strolled out of the palace with his club slung over his shoulders. He was soon back, wearing a lion-skin cloak. He had wrestled the beast to death with his bare hands.

"What next?" asked Heracles, beaming.

"Umm . . . kill the Hydra!" said the surprised king.

The Hydra was a huge, scaly dragon that lived in a vile swamp. It had hundreds of heads, and if one was cut off, it grew back right away. The king was sure he would never see Heracles again. Yet a few weeks later, Heracles strode back into the palace—a little muddy, but alive and well.

"I chopped off the Hydra's heads, then stopped them from growing back by burning the stumps," he explained triumphantly, a big grin on his face.

"Your third task is to capture the sacred hind!" gulped the king, totally amazed.

The sacred hind was a beautiful deer with golden antlers. It could run like the wind, and Heracles spent a whole year tracking it down. Yet he didn't try to capture the deer by force. Instead, he prayed to the goddess Artemis for help, and the graceful animal then trotted obediently behind him all the way back to the king.

The fourth task was to kill an enormous, wild boar that had been roaming the countryside, destroying crops and killing animals. The huge, hairy beast was so scary that when Heracles came staggering back with its dead body across his shoulders, the frightened king ran away and hid.

By this time the goddess Hera was becoming annoyed. *I need something more difficult!* she thought to herself.

Soon, Heracles found himself in the largest, filthiest stables in the world. His awful task was to clean them from top to bottom, all in just one day.

This calls for brains more than muscles, Heracles thought, almost choking from the horrible stench. He dug two channels from the stables to a couple of nearby rivers.

The water flooded down the channels and gushed through the stables, washing them clean in minutes.

For his sixth task, Heracles had to destroy a flock of man-eating birds. They had metal wings and razor-sharp beaks and claws, and they were cunning, too. As soon as the birds saw Heracles coming with his bow, they perched high in the trees with their metal wings folded around them. Heracles' arrows just bounced off them.

The goddess Athena decided that the determined young man deserved some help, so she gave Heracles a special rattle. Every time he shook it, the birds were scared out of the trees. Quick as a flash, Heracles shot his arrows into their soft stomachs and the birds fell dead out of the skies.

Heracles' seventh task was to catch a huge bull belonging to the sea god, Poseidon. The ferocious beast was on the loose, killing anyone who went near it. But it was no match for the mighty Heracles. He soon hauled the struggling bull to the palace.

The eighth task was even more dangerous—to capture some famous flesh-eating horses. Heracles wasn't afraid. He killed the evil horse owner and fed his body to the snarling animals. Then, while the horses gorged, Heracles tied them up and drove them home.

When the king saw the slavering beasts, he cowered behind his throne, overcome with fright.

Next, Heracles was sent into the clutches of a tribe of savage warrior women who battered to death any man they met. But somehow Heracles came back whistling a happy tune, with the bronze armor of the warrior queen swinging from his hand!

When the king told Heracles the tenth task, the hero's eyes lit up. He had to fetch a herd of cows belonging to the giant Geryon. Geryon was famous for having three heads and six arms—but Heracles soon took care of that. He chopped the giant into bits and herded his cattle straight back to the king.

With only two more tasks to go, Hera had a brainstorm. She told the king to order Heracles to fetch the golden apples from the ends of the earth. These magical apples grew in a garden that only the gods were allowed into.

Once again, Heracles outwitted Hera. He tricked a god called Atlas into entering the garden and picking the apples for him.

And Heracles even did an extra task on his way back! The hero stopped to free the god Prometheus, who had been chained up by Zeus as a punishment for having given fire to humans.

Finally Heracles faced his very last task. It was the most difficult and dangerous of all. Alone, he marched down the dark, silent path that led to the underworld, the land of the dead. He seized the brute who guarded the entrance—a three-headed dog called Cerberus, who had a mane of hissing snakes. Heracles closed his ears to the wails of the souls in torment and shrugged off the ghostly fingers that clutched at him from the mists. He dragged the snarling dog back to the king, only to find that the terrified man ran screaming from the room.

At last Heracles had won his prize. He was made a god and went to live on Mount Olympus. And no one ever dared to say that he hadn't earned his place there— not even the jealous Queen Hera.

THE ISLAND OF THE GIANTS

Odysseus was a great explorer. For ten long years he had been sailing the high seas, discovering new lands and meeting strange people.

He and his crew eventually came to a small, rocky island. They were hungry and thirsty, so they jumped ashore and set off to look for food and fresh water.

Suddenly the sky darkened. There was a crash of thunder and a flash of lightning and the clouds poured down raindrops the size of marbles. The men ran for shelter into the nearest cave. They sat there shivering, waiting for the storm to stop.

Suddenly, over the splashing of the rain, the soaked travelers heard bleating and the pattering of hoofs, and a flock of sheep came scrambling into the cave. Then there was a harsh, gravelly noise and the light in the cave was blotted out. Odysseus realized with horror that someone—or something—had rolled a huge boulder across the entrance. They were trapped! The frightened men sat helplessly in the darkness until one by one they fell into an uneasy sleep.

Odysseus and his crew awoke to the noise of the boulder being pushed away and the sheep trotting out.

Daylight flooded the cave entrance for a moment until the figure of a giant stepped into the sunshine. The giant had just one eye, right in the middle of his forehead, and it opened wide in surprise.

"Humans!" the giant grinned. He reached into the cave and grabbed two men, then shoved them into his mouth and swallowed them whole.

"Who are you?" he bellowed at Odysseus, licking his lips. "Where are you from? Are you someone important?"

"No," sighed Odysseus, feeling terrible at having failed to protect his friends.

He certainly didn't feel like a great explorer right then.

"I'm nobody," he said, sadly.

"Well, Nobody," chortled the giant, as he rolled the boulder back in front of the cave. "I shall enjoy eating you!"

Odysseus and his men sat in the darkness all day, trying to think of a way out. Finally the giant returned. He followed his sheep into the cave and then blocked the entrance behind him. Cheerily, the giant built a fire and warmed his huge, hairy hands and feet. Then he grabbed two men and gulped them down greedily with several swigs of wine. Soon he lay snoring in a drunken sleep.

It was the moment Odysseus had been waiting for. He seized a blazing wooden stake from the fire and thrust it into the giant's one eye as hard as he could.

The giant sat up and howled—so loudly that the men thought the roof of the cave would come tumbling down. They shuddered as they heard giant footsteps outside.

"Are you all right in there?" voices boomed.

The giant remembered the name of the bold human who had spoken to him: Nobody.

"Nobody's hurting me!" he moaned.

"Well, then be quiet in there!" laughed the giant's friends, and they went back to their caves.

The blinded giant writhed in pain until morning.

"When my flock are out to graze, I'll take care of you!" he roared at the humans in a fury.

Fumbling around, the giant rolled the rock aside just enough to let his sheep slip through. Then he felt along each animal's woolly back as it went past, to check that it was a sheep and not a human trying to escape.

Imagine the giant's shock when he counted the last sheep and heard Nobody's voice coming from *outside* the cave!

"You should have felt *underneath* your sheep," he laughed. "We were strapped under their stomachs."

The blind giant nearly exploded with fury.

"And by the way, my name is not Nobody," came the voice, disappearing hastily down the mountainside. "It is Odysseus. Remember it well!"

THE WOODEN HORSE

Everyone knew that Helen of Greece was the most beautiful woman in the world. Prince Paris of Troy was determined that she should be his wife. The headstrong young man marched straight off to Greece. He was sure that Helen would be so impressed by his good looks, fine clothes, and sparkling conversation that she would fall helplessly into his arms. Unfortunately the Trojan prince hadn't counted on one thing. Helen was already married, and she was very much in love with her husband.

Still, Paris didn't let a little snag like that put him off. He stole Helen away from Greece and carried her kicking and screaming to Troy. Then the goddess of love, Aphrodite, cast a spell over poor Helen to make her fall head over heels in love with Paris. Helen forgot all about her husband. She had eyes only for Paris.

The Greeks were outraged by the kidnapping and sent a mighty fleet of warships after Paris. All the people of Troy came out to see the splendid sight. The waves glittered with a floating army of hundreds of soldiers!

The Greeks didn't attack right away. First they tried talking to Paris. Then they tried making threats.

The rude prince simply laughed in their faces. Finally the Greeks gave up on words and surrounded the city.

For nine long years the Greek soldiers let no one in and no one out of Troy. Day after day the Trojans faced attacks and water shortages and empty shelves in the food shops. But still they didn't surrender.

Eventually the patient Greeks got tired of waiting. They thought hard and hit upon a master plan. And next morning the Trojan sentries saw an incredible sight. The busy Greek army camp had vanished silently in the night—tents, horses, chariots, soldiers, and all. The Trojans could see the Greek warships far out at sea, sailing away. All that was left was a giant, wooden horse on wheels, towering blankly up to the sky. One by one, the puzzled Trojan people crept out to have a look.

Helen was suspicious. She knew how cunning the Greeks could be.

"Don't have anything to do with it!" she warned people.

But the Trojans didn't listen. They decided the horse was either a peace token or an offering to the gods, and they dragged it triumphantly inside their walls. That evening, there was feasting like never before.

"We've won the war!" the people cried. "The cowardly Greeks have gone home!"

Everyone was having far too much fun to notice the Greek ships turn back to Troy and land on the beach. When all the Trojans had fallen happily into their beds, something began to stir in the hollow belly of the wooden horse. There had been Greek soldiers hiding in it all along, keeping as still and silent as statues. Now they opened a trap door and climbed out right into the middle of Troy. The soldiers threw open the gates and the Greek army streamed in, taking the sleeping city totally by surprise.

The Trojans didn't stand a chance, and by morning their mighty city was burned to the ground. The surprise present had turned out to be a deadly trick!

Jason and the Golden Fleece

Jason was the rightful king of Iolcus, but his evil uncle had seized the throne.

"I will let you become king," his uncle promised with a wicked grin, "if you bring me the Golden Fleece."

Now, Jason loved a challenge—and finding the Golden Fleece was possibly the greatest challenge of them all. The fleece was the woolly coat of a magical ram, and it lay far away at the end of the world.

The clever young warrior prepared himself well. First he ordered a huge boat to be built, strong enough to face all dangers. Jason called it the *Argo*. Then he sent messages far and wide to Heracles, Theseus, and all the other famous heroes in Greece. Before long Jason had the bravest crew the world had ever seen.

The morning the heroes sailed, all the people of Iolcus came to cheer them as they set off on their dangerous voyage. The crowd waved until the *Argo* disappeared over the edge of the world. They wondered if they would ever see Jason and his friends again.

For many months, the *Argo* sailed tirelessly across the sea. Jason and his mighty crew visited many lands.

As tales spread of their adventures, they became known as the Argonauts.

Eventually they came to Thrace, the home of King Phineus. The king was old and blind, but people swore he could see into the future. Jason wanted to ask Phineus for advice on finding the Golden Fleece.

They found the king pale and thin and close to death. Every day, terrifying winged women called Harpies swooped down and stole his food, leaving him starving. The Argonauts chased the Harpies away, and in return the grateful king told Jason many helpful things....

The brave Argonauts set sail again, ready to face the next danger. King Phineus had warned them that they had to pass between two towering cliffs that would smash together and crush them to pieces. The king had told Jason what he must do to avoid this terrible fate.

Following the king's instructions, Jason released a dove and watched as it flew toward the cliffs. Suddenly the huge cliffs smashed together, but the dove flew so fast that only a few of its tail feathers were trapped.

"We must row as fast as the dove flew!" Jason shouted to his crew. "If we don't, we will be crushed to pieces!"

The heroes gritted their teeth and strained at the oars until the water churned white around the speeding ship.

The Argonauts rowed faster than any crew except the gods could row. And when the cliffs clashed together, only the very tip of the *Argo* was caught between them. The sweating, panting heroes breathed a huge sigh of relief. There was only a handful of small splinters floating past them on the tide.

Finally, the Argonauts reached the city of Colchis—the home of the Golden Fleece itself.

"Welcome!" King Aeëtes greeted the Argonauts politely. But there was a cold glint in his eye.

"I hear you have come for my Golden Fleece, Jason," the king continued. "Well, I'll be honored to give it to such a brave hero. But only on one condition. Tomorrow you must hitch my two fire-breathing bulls to a plow and sow my field with dragons' teeth."

The Argonauts gasped. Surely the task was impossible!

"See you in the morning," the king chuckled cruelly.

Jason might well have failed, if the king's daughter Medea hadn't secretly paid him a visit that night. She had fallen deeply in love with the bold hero.

"Promise you will take me back to Greece as your wife," Medea urged, "and I will help you win the Golden Fleece."

Jason quickly agreed, and the joyful girl gave him a magic ointment to rub all over his skin.

"Just for one day, this will keep you safe from all fire and weapons," Medea whispered.

Next morning, King Aeëtes was amazed to see Jason harness the fire-breathing bulls to the plow without singeing as much as a hair on his head. Jason urged the beasts forward and plowed the field. Then he sowed the dragons' teeth into the earth. Moments later, the enchanted seeds sprang up into an army of soldiers that came marching at Jason like unstoppable machines!

Thinking quickly, Jason used an old trick. He picked up a stone and flung it at the back of a soldier's head. Angrily, the soldier spun around and accused the man behind of hitting him. A fight broke out, and in a few moments all the soldiers were slashing each other with their swords. Soon they all lay in a lifeless heap.

"Bravo, Jason," congratulated the king between gritted teeth. "Tomorrow you shall have the Golden Fleece."

That night Medea again slipped into Jason's room.

"Do not believe my father," the love-struck girl warned. "He plans to burn your ship and kill you all. If you want the Golden Fleece, you must follow me now."

Jason gratefully crept into the darkness after Medea. She led him to a grove of trees. Jason gasped. There was the glittering Golden Fleece, hanging from a branch!

Then his face fell. At the foot of the tree lay a huge dragon, its tail curled around the trunk a thousand times. The dragon opened its mighty jaws, flicked its forked tongue, and hissed at Jason.

Medea just smiled. She began to sing a soothing spell, and the dragon's scaly eyelids started to droop. Bravely, Medea stepped forward and sprinkled sleeping dust into the dragon's eyes. It fell into an enchanted sleep. Jason's heart pounded as he pulled the Golden Fleece from the branch. Then the couple raced with their precious prize all the way to the silvery shore where the Argonauts were waiting at their ship.

"Home," Jason sighed. "It's time to go home...."

INDEX